1

William Bingham Meade

My Story of the

Battle of the Cowpens

January 17, 1781

Written by:

Elaine Meade Meddings

Published by:

Wiltshire Books LLC

Huntington, West Virginia

Published by:

Wiltshire Books LLC

Huntington, West Virginia

ISBN—978-0-9970240-6-7

Copyright © 2016

First Printing 2016

*C*owpens *B*attlefield

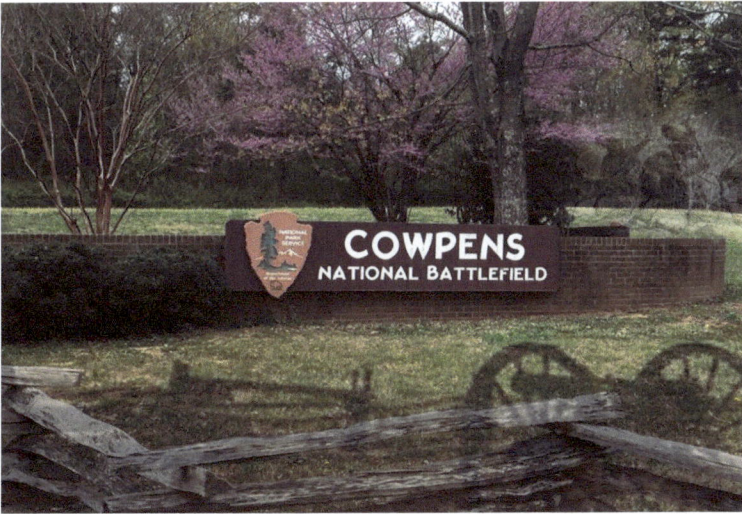

Elaine Meddings 2016

William and his family moved from Frederick County Virginia to Logan County Virginia (now West Virginia) then in 1793 they settled at Fort Vancouver which is situated on the point section and connects the Levisa River in Kentucky and the Tug River in West Virginia to make the Big Sandy River. In 1801 they then moved to Marrowbone Creek, Mingo County, West Virginia. According to his pension letter, at the age of fifty, William enlisted in the War of 1812 where he served his country again at Fort Defiance as a wagon master in the Gray Beard Company. In 1836, at the age of 74, William moved to Indiana to live with his son William Bingham Meade Jr., but then moved back to West Virginia where he died at the age of 79 years old.

The Meade Family lives on today and with their help, my story lives on as well. It is my hope, with the telling of my story of the Battle of Cowpens, that others will realize how important this small battle was to our great nation.

About This Book . . .

This is the story of my fourth great-grandfather, **William Bingham Meade**. He volunteered in the military for as long as he was permitted and then, at the age of sixteen, enlisted in Wilks County, North Carolina. He served his country as a private in the Revolutionary War as a member of the 5th Regiment commanded by Lt. Colonel John Edgar Howard and then fought under Captain George Baker, Colonel Daniel Morgan and Colonel Andrew Pickens.

During the battle of The Cowpens, William was on the front line as a skirmisher, after firing his two shots as ordered, he reloaded his gun and continued to fight. He received several severe wounds, including being hit in the head by a saber, causing him to have five pieces of his skull removed. He was bayonetted in the leg and right breast and had several ribs broken. He was stripped naked and left for dead. However, William was found alive and treated on the battlefield, which allowed him to be able to march to Gilbert Town, North Carolina where he was admitted to the hospital under the care of their surgeons. William remained in the hospital for eight months and was then released in September of 1781. In 1786, at the age of twenty-four, Captain George Baker signed his discharge from service.

William returned to Wilkes County, North Carolina and married Miss Mildred Ester Davis (1769-1830) on December 30, 1787. The couple had eight children: Elizabeth Meade (1789-1870), Samuel Meade (1791-1869), Ann Meade (1794-1830), William Bingham Meade, Jr. (1798-1883), Keziah Meade (1805-1844), John Meade (1810-1878), France Sofana Meade (1814-1876) and Margaret Meade (1817-1893).

I would like to o dedicate this book to Jamie and Sue.
Thanks girls for traveling with me to take the pictures.
(Even though it was just a few stops on the way to the
beach.)

Also, to John Hash for his wealth of knowledge
about the Meade family. Thank you for taking the time
to help.

Finally, this book is dedicated to William Meade,
my 4th great grandfather, for without him, I would not
be.

Elaine

My Story Begins...

On August 22, 1762, I was born in Frederick County, Virginia. Frederick County was formed from parts of Orange County in 1743 and it was named for the Prince of Wales, Frederick Louis (1707-1751). Frederick was the eldest son of King George II of Britain.

King George III
Portrait by Johann Zoffany
Wikimedia Public Domain

It was the year 1778 and I was sixteen years old, just like any other boy, I though I would conquer the world. I had heard talk of the political and military disasters that plagued the people in our country. There were people who were rebelling against King George III.

Each day we would hear news of how the British commanders were winning over the people and their

George Washington
Portrait by Gilbert Stuart
Wikimedia Public Domain

lands either willingly or by force. Now, with new tactics, the British would leave enough troops in hopes to slow down George Washington's army which was near New York and then the British would send more of their troops to take over places like Charleston, South Carolina and other cities and surrounding areas. General Benjamin Lincoln and the city of

General Benjamin Lincoln
painted by Charles
Willson Peale
Wikimedia Public Domain

Charleston, South Carolina surrendered to the British on May 12, 1780 and with that

Cowpens Battlefield

surrender we lost thousands of muskets, a number of cannons, tons of gunpowder and hundreds of other important military supplies along with personnel that were either captured or killed. This was the worst defeat of the war.

Cowpens Battlefield

Hearing all of this, I knew what I had to do. At the time, I was living in Wilkes County, North Carolina, so in September of 1778 I volunteered my services to the military. I was quickly involved in several skirmishes with the British.

I was hearing the people talk, they were saying thing like, there were thousands of British troops and they had plenty of weapons and ammunition and we did not have an army in either North or South Carolina that was strong enough to defeat the British troops. After all, Savanna, Georgia had been con-quered on December 29, 1778 and Charleston, South Carolina surren-

Cowpens Battlefield

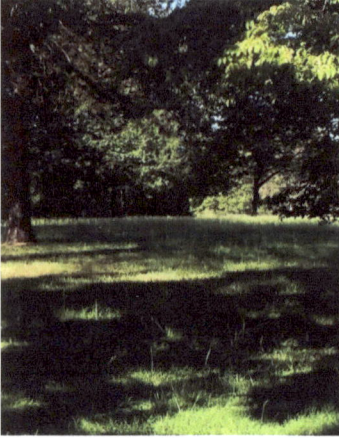

Cowpens Battlefields

dered on May of 1780. By late summer of that year, it was ru-mored that General Cornwallis was ready to sweep in to the Carolinas and cross on into Virginia. We were hearing that there were American loyalists that believed their rights would be better protected if they swore an oath of allegiance to the King. Times were looking grim!

I was only sixteen years old but I knew it was my duty as an American to serve my country any way I could.

So, I first volunteered under Captain William Thomas' militia and was with him for six months before my time as a volunteer expired. I then enlisted in the Continental line of the Army of the Revolution as a Private in the company commanded by Captain George Baker in the regiment commanded by Colonel Benjamin Cleveland of Wilkes County North Carolina.

Battle of Kettle Creek Feb. 14, 1779

Colonel Cleveland was said to

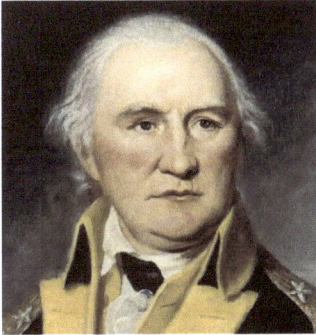

Daniel Morgan by Charles Willson Peale, 1794 Independence National Historical Park Public Domain

be from Virginia. After the skirmishes with the British and the Tories, while serving under Captain George Baker, I was called to the aid of Brigadier General Daniel Morgan to fight in the Virginia line.

General Morgan was a 6'2" frontiersman with a full round face, blue eyes and dark hair. He was called, respectfully, Old Waggoneer by his troops and his veterans. Morgan respected his troops and they also had the upmost respect for him and he led them by example and they followed him willingly. His men were made up of three types of soldiers: the militia, the Continentals, and the state troops. Morgan took command of General Nathanael.

Nathanael Greene by Charles Willson Peale 1783 Wikimedia Public Domain

Lt.Colonel John Edgar Howard painted in 1782 by Charles Willson Peale Wikimedia Public Domain

Greene's troops in 1780. Nathanael Greene was born on July 27, 1742. He loved to read and save money. He was also one of the most trusted generals in the Army. He was also a good friend of George Washington.

After my time with Brigadier General Morgan, I was put under the command of Lieutenant Colonel John Edgar Howard who obeyed the orders of General Greene, you see, because General Morgan was growing sicker by the day. He suffered from a condition caused by rheumatic inflammation of the sciatic nerve in his hip, which made riding his horse very painful, and the long days just made his condition worse.

After my time with Lieutenant Colonel Howard, I was left in the care of General Andrew Pickens. You Often heard the Cherokee call General Pickens the Wizard Owl.

Andrew Pickens from Wikipedia, the free Encyclopedia Photo of Oil Painting by - blahedo

They feared General Pickens but they also honored and respected him. General Pickens was born in Bucks County, Pennsylvania and was married to Rebecca Calhoun. They lived along the Long Cane Creek settlement in the Ninety Six

Rebecca Calhoun
Anonymous Brown WikiTree

District of South Carolina. The area consisted of about 12 or 14 houses, a court-house ,and a jail and about 100 to 150 people lived in the area along the creek.

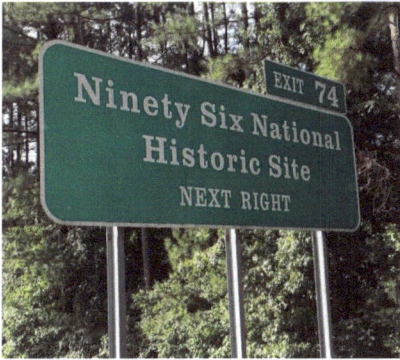

The Ninety Six District

After the Siege of Charles-ton where he surrendered a fort in the Ninety Six District, he along with about 300 militia men swore on an oath to sit out the war and went home on parole, but about 1800 Torie raiders came along and destroyed much of his property and terrorized his family. After that General Pickens told the British commanders they had violated the terms of their agreement and rejoined the war. General Andrew Pickens was a 41 year old man and stood 6 feet tall. Andrew Pickens was a quiet man and he tried to stay peaceful as long as possible, but eventually had to make the decision to call out his regiment. Unfortunately, when he called only a few men came out, possibly because they had joined other groups so they could continue to fight.

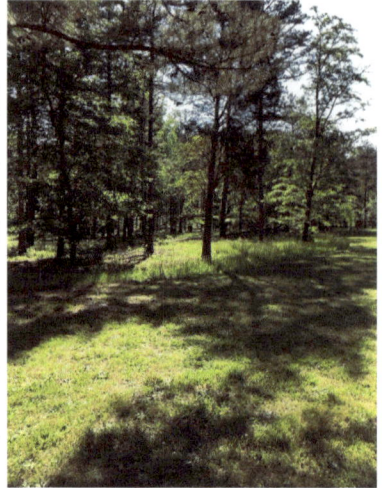

Cowpens Battlefield

Morgan gave Pickens command of the Militia. He knew that Pickens and his men knew the back country well and he could use them as his eyes and ears to slip quietly through the thick forest and thru the water ways. He also knew that Pickens and his men would be beneficial in helping to move about most of the creeks and marshy land as it would be difficult to get through the terrain without some experience.

Our orders were to rendezvous at the Wilkes County Court House and then march from there to our encampment which was about four miles from the Cowpens, near the Cross Roads. It was there where we would fight Banastre Tarleton.

Banastre Tarleton was twenty-one years old when he came to America. He had bright red hair, thick shoulders, and was of average height. He was born on Water Street in Liverpool, England.

Most of the American troops who knew Tarleton or had heard of him, especially the southern troops, feared and hated him. Tarleton, though lacking in experience, had exceptional abilities some equal to those of Daniel Morgan. Most of the American troops nicknamed him the Butcher or Bloody Tarleton. Daniel Morgan's favorite name for him was Benny!

Tarleton liked to fight at night, he also liked to surprise his enemies, but he would never lead an attack but you could always see him in the background until the fighting started. In the fall of 1776, he played a key roll in capturing Major General Charles Lee, which was the second in command in the American Army.

After the war, Tarleton fell in love with Mary Robinson, a poet, playwright and actress. Mary was born on November 27, 1758. Mary was third in line of five children. She loved poetry as a child.

Mary Robinson Thomas Gainsborough Wikimedia Public Domain Created 31 December 1780

Mary received her first proposal by the age of 13 and was married to Thomas Robinson on April 12, 1774. They had a daughter, Maria Elizabeth on November 18, 1774. Thomas, Mary and the baby lived in a debtors prison for over a year. Mary's most famous role was Perdita in "A Winters Tale."

Cowpens Battlefield

Tarleton won a bet with Lord Malden, Mary's protector, that he could seduce Mary. When Mary found out about the bet she was furious with both men. Lord Malden rejected her after she betrayed him. Tarleton and Mary's relationship lasted 15 years until 1798.

By that time Tarleton became interested in politics and became a member of Parliament. Mary continued to write and she achieved considerable acclaim. After Tarleton's mothers death in 1797 he ended his relationship with Mary and married an Heiress, Susan Priscilla Bertie. Mary died on December 26, 1800.

Cowpens Battlefield

Morgan knew that his military forces were inadequate, he did not have enough men to compare to the British nor did we have sufficient guns or cannons to use that would compare to the ones we would be fighting against and after getting multiple reports of a large legion of British Troops coming at us.

Morgan's in his mind knew what he must do, he would prepare for the inevitable- to fight as long as possible, but he would also, prepare for surrender. He had been in too many battles and he had to much

Cowpens Battlefield

experience not to be prepared for what happen, especially since he had been getting information that Tarleton's forces included eleven to, twelve hundred British soldiers.

Cowpens Battlefield

At the time of the Cowpens conflict, Banaster Tarleton was only twenty-six years old, he was well trained and had experience in battles, but Morgan who was older and was an experienced Indian fighter and frontiersman had some tactics of his own that Tarleton would have never seen coming at him.

Cowpens Battlefield

On the morning of January 16, 1781 we were getting reports that Tarleton was just a few miles down the river from our location. This was not a good thing. As soon as General Morgan heard the news he rushed out of his tent and ordered us to prepare to move out immediately. It was early in

Cowpens Battlefield

the morning and we were fixing breakfast, so in a rush we grabbed what we could of our half cooked food and ran for our horses. The waggoneers hitched up their teams and we gathered up what belonging we had and moved out, toward the Cowpens, on the Green

Cowpens Battlefield

River Road. We were trying to get to the Island Ford which crossed the Broad River, about six miles beyond Cowpens, but it was raining and slick, and the roads were gooey with mud, and this made marching for us hard to

Cowpens Battlefield

do. As we marched, we eventually came upon a large pasture that the locals called "The Cowpens", because that is where they would feed their cattle before they drove them to market.

As Morgan looked over this large pasture, he saw thick woods on both sides. The land would roll and dip and then flatten out and then all of a sudden there would be another rise and fall of the land and then it would roll into a hollow. Part of the land had streams and some swampy places. Things were starting to look promising as far as slowing down the British troops.

Morgan was in hopes hey could reach the Blue Ridge

The Blue Ridge Mountains   Elaine Meddings 2016

Mountains, which were about thirty miles away. He thought that reaching the mountains might keep him and his men safe, and it would be a better location also if hey had to fight the British.

The Cowpens was a junction in the road and it was familiar to both the British and the Americans. At this intersection

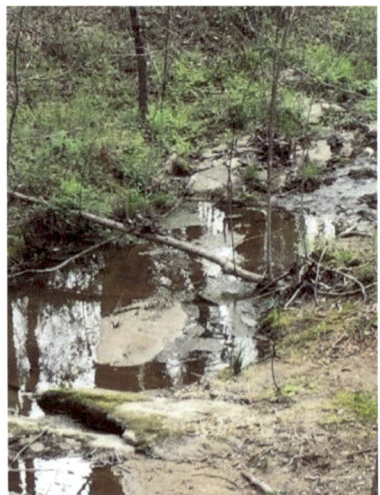

Cowpens Battlefield

the road provided access to the Green River Road, which was located at the north end of the Cowpens. It also provided access to other river crossings such as Broad River's Island Ford which was five miles to the northeast and Coulter Ford across the

Green River Road
Elaine Meddings 2016

Pacolet River, which was five miles to the west.

Jul 13, 2016
Shared with Shoebox

The Broad River

As Morgan and the leaders of the militia men were devising plans of a possible ambush of the British, it was mentioned that Cowpens with all the possible coverage and hiding places and the trails and streams it would be a good place to fight.

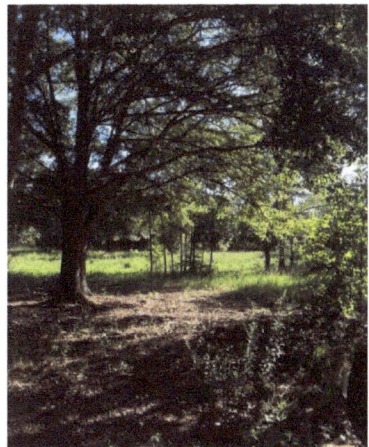

Cowpens Battlefield

At this time Captain Whiteside and some of his men's enlistment time had expired. Knowing this Morgan appealed to Captain Whiteside to please stay until fresh troops could arrive. Knowing that we were about to go to battle he agreed to stay.

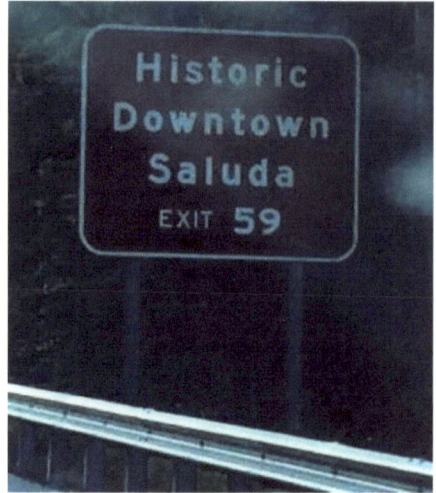

Historic Marker
Elaine Meddings 2016

We were about six miles away from Island Ford, a shallow crossing of the Saluda River; It had been raining and the water was rising and things looked pretty gloomy. As Morgan looked around, he began to realize that this would be a pretty good place to fight Tarleton. As he scanned the area, he realized there would be cover from the thick trees and the gradual rise and fall and rise again into a higher crest of land. It was perfect! Morgan was happy with what he saw.

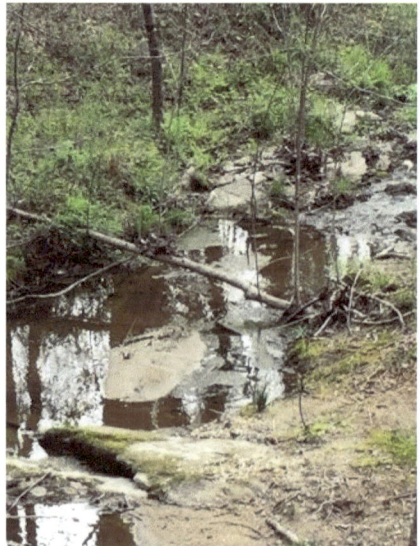

Cowpens Battlefield

Tarleton was told by his spies that Morgan had about 3,000 men. Expecting an attack from the patriots, the British barricaded themselves on the north bank of the Pacolet River in a log cabin.

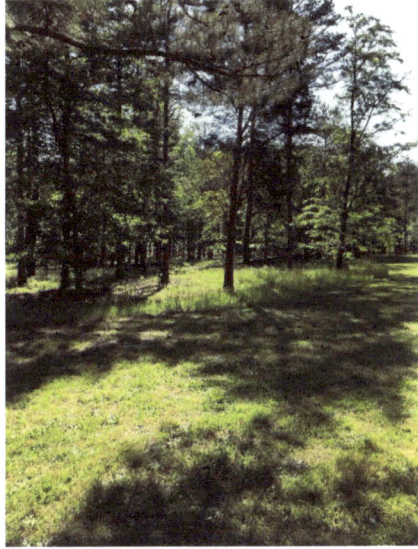
Cowpens Battlefield

Morgan, on the other hand, was in the process of ordering a retreat. Soon after the first reports, Tarleton was alerted that Morgan was breaking camp and moving out. This angered Tarleton and made his blood boiling! He thought that Morgan was running from him so he Immediately moved his men into Morgan's abandoned

Cowpens Battlefield

campsite. Tarleton's men were wet, tired and hungry and glad to find the half cooked food Morgan's men had left behind. In Tarleton's mind, the sudden move by Morgan meant a retreat and considered this to be an easy victory.

Cowpens Battlefield

This was not just a feeling but it was how he had been trained. He immediately sent spies to observe the American troops. He was after Morgan and his men. And just because he thought Morgan was retreating he wasn't. going to give up an easy victory. He was going after them.

Cowpens Battlefield

Early in the morning of January 16, a colonel who was out looking for food and water for his horse had dropped out of the American line of marching. He was spotted some British troops and captured, and taken back to Tarleton. After being questioned, the soldier told Tarleton that he thought Morgan was going to stop at the Cowpens. As the hours passed, Tarleton kept getting reports of Morgan getting reinforcements. Tarleton was infuriated by these reports.

Cowpens Battlefield

The next day, January 17, 1781 the morning started out cold, cloudy, and humid in South Carolina. The sunrise was to come at about 7:36 a.m. Earlier that morning we had scouts out on horseback when all of a sudden they collided with some British forces. Two of our scouts were captured and taken back to Tarleton's camp. After being questioned by Tarleton's forces, they told that Morgan was located only a few miles away at the Cowpens. Tarleton called his troops out to march.

Marching in the dark was not going to be an easy task for Tarleton because there were creeks, marshes, and ravines. On top of that, *Cowpens Battlefield* the woods were thick and it was hard to see where you were marching. Even in the middle of the day there was shade that made it hard to see.

It was cold and we were always looking around to

prevent being ambushed by the British.   As the morning dark turned into light, Tarleton sent some of his troops out to find the location of Morgan's camp. Then he ordered more troops out, one group at a time. Tarleton's men marched on for what seemed like hours. At this point not finding Morgan, Tarleton was sure that he was retreating.

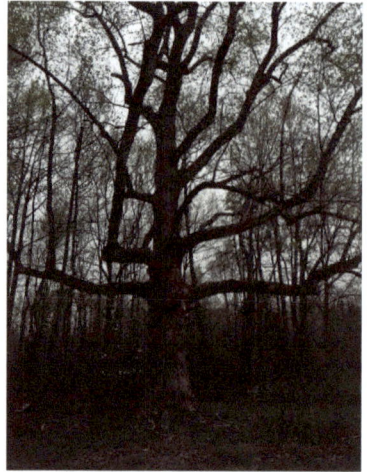

Cowpens Battlefield

Suddenly, one of Tarleton's men came rushing back to tell him that Morgan was not retreating and Tarleton instantly knew that Mor-

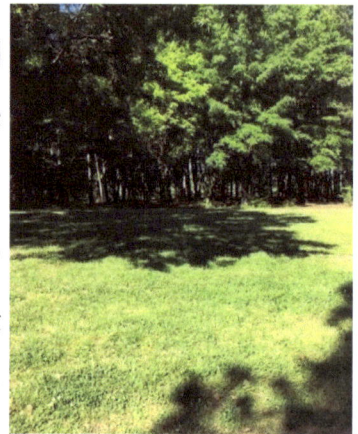

Cowpens Battlefield

gan had chosen a place to fight. It was going to be at the Cowpens. Although Tarleton didn't know the layout of the land his guides gave him a detailed description.

His guides told him that there was flat land and some wooded areas but that they were open and fairly flat with some trees but that it were free from swamps. They also told him that the river was about six miles away.

Cowpens Battlefield

Morgan's men were crack shots and he knew that Tarleton would come straight at them, that's the way the British would fight. Bu-tut it was our custom in militia warfare to hide behind trees and rocks so not to be readily seen and so that we could shelter our bodies and we could fire from the side.

Morgan also knew that his men couldn't stand up to a bay-onet charge from the British, so Morgan's battle plan was to use his best men up front, so he sta-tioned Andrew Pickens men on each side of the first crest of land. Then he planned to post his eighty dragoons, which were

Cowpens Battlefield

more of a match for Tarleton's 300 horsemen behind them. Morgan was selecting the best area for his infantry to be placed so that they could protect themselves and Washington's cavalry from immediate danger of

Cowpens Battlefield

Tarleton's many horsemen. He was then planning on placing his backwoodsmen in a line of about 150 yards of the Continentals. They were to hold their fire until the British were within range, then fire two shots and then retreat behind the Continentals until they could reload and come back to fight.

Just at the crack of daylight Morgan sent out some of his cavalry to scout the area for the British. While out, our men bumped into some of Tarleton's men, so Morgan's boys hastily retreated and rode back into camp shouting the alarm. Morgan jumped up and started running around and using his favorite name for Tarleton started screaming "He's coming He's coming, Benny's on his way!" He sent out the picked

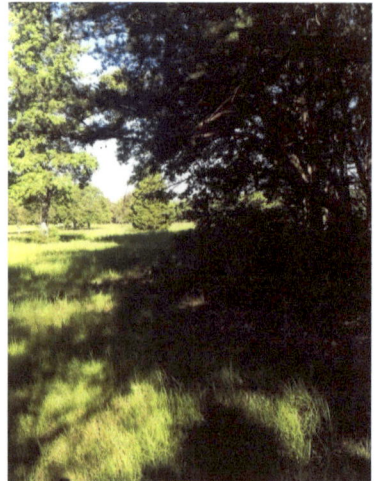
Cowpens Battlefield

riflemen who were going to open the fight. This was my

location. We were known as skirmishers and we were from Georgia, North Carolina and South Carolina and by being on the front line it was our job to open the fight. Morgan's plans were to put the Carolina men on the right side (again this is where I was placed) and the

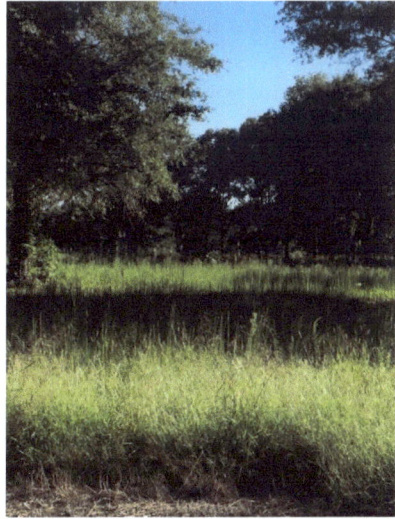

Cowpens Battlefield

Georgia men was on the left side. Morgan thought by doing this there would be competition between us you know how young men are some times and this competition would be highly visible because we would try to out do the others and General Morgan knew our attitudes were crucial to the success of the battle. At one point in the day General Morgan thought about crossing into North Carolina but if Morgan had crossed the river into North Carolina at that earlier point that day, he would have lost the South Carolina Militiamen. This would have been devastating to us because they made up more that half of our forces. You see, they were upset because they thought by doing this, we were retreating to avoid a fight.

Morgan knew that they were anxious for battle and they would be excited when they realized they were going to get to fight after all.

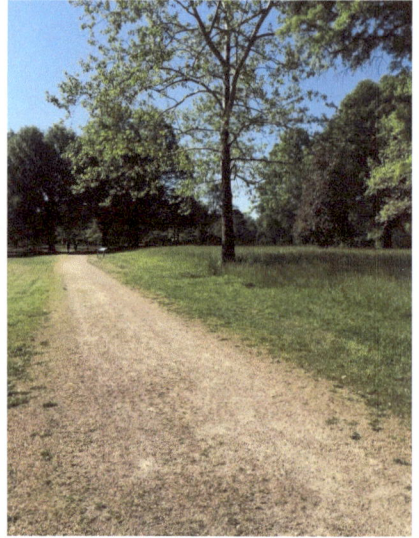

Cowpens Battlefield

The day was brisk and cold. The red sun rose over the mountain. We were stomping our feet and rubbing our hands together just trying to stay warm. Our blood was rushing so hard through our veins we could almost feel it and our hearts were beating so hard that I could swear you could almost hear it. We were excited and feeling pretty good that morning. Morgan came around to reassure each of us the night before that we could do this and he made sure we had plenty of rest also and food was plentiful too. With us being at the Cowpens, where the farmers brought their cattle to graze

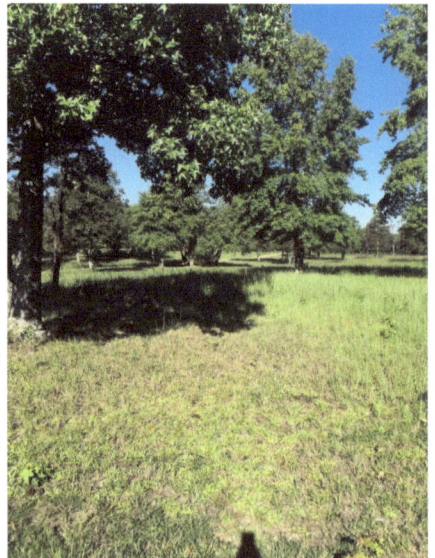

Cowpens Battlefield

before they took them to market, this was convenient because it made it possible for us to have cattle to butcher for food. He also made sure that we had plenty of ammunition. He was stipulating the number of bullets each person was given, so that he could count the shots and know how long we could fight before we ran out to re-

Cowpens Battlefield

load our gun.

All of a sudden we heard several pops of a rifle. Then in the next instant we saw the British. The first ones we saw was the green-coated dragoons that rode up and stopped. Nest, behind them it was the red-coated light infantry. After that, ol'Banastre Tarleton rode up to the front of the line. As he set on his horse he studied our line. As he looked it over, he found it was quite dangerous. But he couldn't see our militia line or even see the right flank of men. And the left flank of riflemen in the woods,

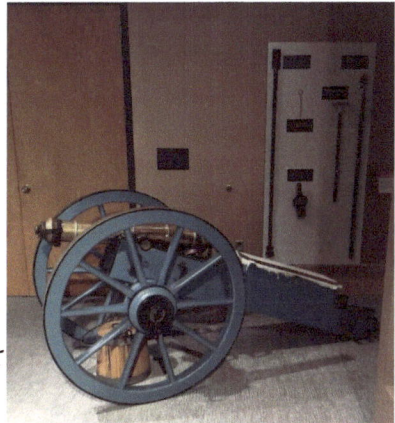

Cowpens Battlefield

those from Georgia, could only partially be seen.

I was nineteen years old at the time and I was a private on the front line of this battle as a skirmisher when the fighting started. I got my two shots off and withdrew to reload and continued to

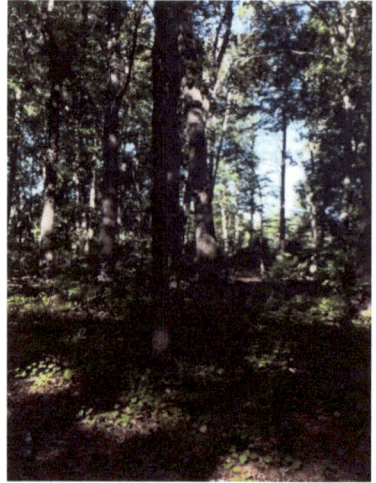

Cowpens Battlefield

fight with the right flank as the militia line retreated. Even with the poor light and visibility, Tarleton turned and ordered "drive in". As we steadied our rifles against the trees and started to fire, we could hear the cries from the dragoons as they were being hit by our shots. We were told to take two shots then retreat back behind the line for safety so we could reload and then to run back out and

fight more. Our orders were to aim low and pick out the British officers with gold braid on their shoulders. The muskets we were using were not accurate for more than fifty yards and it was hard to hold our fire. Our hearts were

Cowpens Battlefield

pounding and we were so excited and scared. We could see their shiny bayonets coming toward us. They were raised up, the sun glistening on the razor sharp blades.

Cowpens Battlefield

"Fire" Pickens shouted the order that signaled the moment of death we had all been fearing. The shot echoed through the field. At first you could hear the sound of the rifles . .

Cowpens Battlefield

. "Pop!...Pop!...Pop!..."Then a whole volley fire, which was designed more to intimidate rather than kill, began. When we looked up, we saw the British charging out of the smoke with their bayonets leveled at us. We fired and shot at them again, then we retreated for our horses, trying to get to the safety of Howard's Continentals, but the British followed. They were swinging their sabers and we were dodging behind trees and using our rifles to stop the slashing of the blades.

35

The British fired a volley, it was very loud which caused confusion. We heard several misunderstood orders and confused commands that led to their execution going wrong. It could have been because of all the noise, the drums, the shouting or

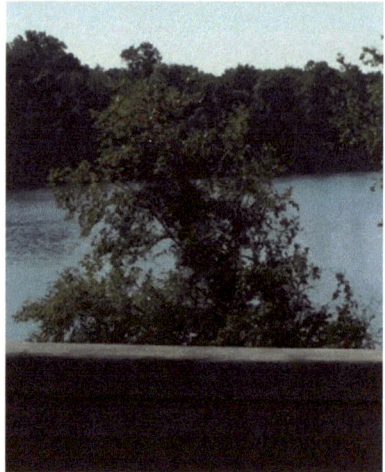

The Broad River

just the sound of gun fire or maybe in our excitement we

Cowpens Battlefield

just heard the commands wrong. We were told to move back, but it appeared to the British as if we were retreating and they thought that they had won the battle. Just then, Morgan ordered an "about face." I think that was the moment when I was hit in my leg and badly wounded by the stroke of a British Lieutenants cutlass . I fell to the ground in agony, but managed to get back up. I tried to get my faculties together, but by that time my I was hit in my right breast with the point of a Highlanders bayonet and that broke several of my ribs. Then I was hit in the head and my skull was fractured by a saber sword. That put me down again, not knowing if I would live or die right there on the battlefield. I was then slashed again by the stroke

Cowpens Battlefield

of a cutlass carried by the hands of the enemy. Assuming I was dead, they stripped me of my clothing and left me lying on the battlefield. The fighting continued and it was brutal, yet a short fight. It only lasted about five minutes or so.

The British thought we had retreated, but as a fact we were just moving a little farther to the right rear, into the boggy grounds of Maple Swamp. It was there that we

Cowpens Battlefield

could continue our battle and fire at long range. We did a pretty good job of covering the right flank and we bought them just enough time for an American victory. It was a short battle as battles go, but it was an important one.

GILBERT TOWN
Established in 1779.
The first county seat
of Rutherford County.
Also the first county
seat in Western North
Carolina. Named for
William Gilbert.

The First Courthouse

It felt like it lasted for days! had to move quickly after the British defeat at Cowpens. He wasn't sure where Cornwallis' location was or if he was being followed by Morgan.

Tarleton was rushing to cross the Broad River at Hamilton's Ford in hopes he could find Cornwallis' camp. But several of his troops refused to cross the flooded river. But he drew his sword then he threatened any one who hesitated to cross. After hearing of the defeat, Cornwallis also knew General Leslie and his army had arrived so he decided to go after Morgan to get his 600 soldiers back, but took a wrong turn and never found Morgan.

Cowpens Battlefield

One priority after the battle was to go after Tarleton, this was done by William Washington, George Washington's cousin. They pursued Tarleton southeastward but lost him when he took a wrong turn. Another concern of Morgan's was, after the battle there was the possibility of the loyalist militia, who might be scouting the area for the British.

Forty-eight hours after the Battle of Cowpens was a crucial time for Morgan and Tarleton. Both trying to cross the Dan River, planning their next moves, with the next battle loom-

Cowpens Battlefields 2016

ing, "the Battle of Guilford Courthouse", where Cornwallis would lose men and officers. Finally he gave up on the Carolinians and headed toward Virginia where he also was de- feated at York Town on October 19 1781.

After the battle, General Morgan gave orders for the wounded to be cared for and the dead to be buried. I was found alive and received treatment at the home of Dr. Robert Nelson. There was a lot of plundering of those that had lost their lives, for an officer's sword was a prize, and there were numerous wounded on both sides that had to be treated. Along with the wounded and the dead, there were prisoners that had to be secured and the weapons and ammunition had to be collected. That night, we camped at the Island Ford and then I began the next day com-

Cowpens Battlefield

pleting my march to Gilbert Town, North Carolina, which was about twenty miles from the Cowpens battle ground. There was a makeshift hospital set up in a tavern across from the home of the William Gilbert family. There was a British doctor on duty as well as a Dr. John Pindell, an American doctor. It was there that the surgeons took care of me. They removed five pieces of bone from my skull. I remained in the hospital for eight months and these wounds disabled me for life.

On February 8th, Daniel Morgan was granted permission to leave the army to recover because of the wounds on both sides of his body that he received during the battle the Cowpens.

Marrowbone Creek, West Viginia

You see, he too was loaded onto a wagon and brought to Gilbert Town with the rest of those hurt in the battle. The Cowpens battle is not a wel-known battle, but is was a very important one, it was a turning point in the Revolutionary War that has often been referred to as a tactical masterpiece.

Three years was the period of my service, including my confinement in the hospital, which was until September 1781. In January of 1786, I received my discharged at the age of 24 years. It was signed by Captain George Baker. After the war, I went back to Wilkes County and married Miss Mildred Ester Davis (1769-1830) on December 30, 1878. We had eight children: Elizabeth Meade (1789-1870) who married Isaac Brewer on May 30,1830 in Logan County, Virginia; Samuel Meade (1791-1869) who married Julia Ann Patton; Ann Meade (1794-1830) who married Perry Burgess; William Bingham Meade Jr. (1798-1883) who married Jane Ellen Rutherford on September 14, 1823 in Pike County, Kentucky. Then we moved to Marrow-bone Creek, Virginia (Now West Virginia in 1801. Then Mildred and I had two more children Keziah Meade (1805-1844) who married John Cline on October 16, 1822 in Pike County, Kentucky; John Meade (1810-1878) who married Sarah Earwood in 1830 in Greenup County, Kentucky.

I enlisted in the War of 1812 and fought at Fort Defiance in 1813. I was a wagon master in the Gray Beard Company at the age of 50 years old.

Between 1813 and 1814 we moved to Fleming County, Kentucky. Then Mildred and I had another daughter Frances Sofana Meade (1814-1876) who married Theophilus Hendricks Goodwin on January 8, 1833 in Greenup County, Kentucky.

On March 13, 1815 the war ended. Then Mildred and I had our last child, Margaret Meade (1817-1893) who married Thomas Bennett Watts on February 7, 1837 in Jennings County, Indiana.

Then in 1830 my beloved wife Mildred Ester passed away at the age of 61. I moved to Greenup County,

Kentucky. At that time I lived close to my sister Elizabeth Meade Cooper, who was married to Robert Cooper and her daughter Jane Cooper Felton. Then in 1834 I move to Cabell County, Virginia (now West Virginia). I then moved again in 1836 at the age of 74 to Indiana with my son, William Bingham Meade Jr.

In 1840 my daughter Keziah Meade died at the age of 35. Then I moved back to Marrowbone Creek, Mingo County, West Virginia and died in 1841 at the age of 79 years old.

My son Samuel Meade died in 1869 at the age of 78 and my daughter Elizabeth Meade died in 1870 at the age of 81, my daughter Frances Sofana Meade died in 1874 at the age of 63, and my son John died in 1878 at the age of 68, my daughter Margaret Meade died in 1893 at the age of 76 and my son William Bingham Meade Jr. died on April 14, 1883 at the age of 84.

TIME LINE for William Bingham Meade Sr.	
William Bingham Meade Sr. was born	Aug 22, 1762
William B. enlisted in the service at 16 yrs old	September, 1778
William B. was wounded he was 19 yrs old	January, 1781
William B. stayed in the hospital 8 months 19 yrs old	September, 1781
William B. was discharged from service at age 24 yrs old	January, 1786
William B. married Mildred Ester Davis. She was born 1769 & died 1830. He was 25 yrs old.	December, 1787
His daughter Elizabeth Meade was born 1789-1870. William was 27 yrs old.	Oct 4, 1789
He moved to Ft. Vancover at the forks of Sandy and Tug. He was 28 yrs old.	1790
His son Samuel Meade was born. 1791-1869. William was 29 yrs old.	1791
His daughter Ann Meade was born. 1795 - ?? William was 33 yrs old.	1795
His Son William Bingham Meade Jr. was born. 1798-1902. William was 36 yrs old.	April 25, 1798
His son John Meade was born. 1800 - ??. William was 38 yrs old.	1800
They moved to Marrowbone WV in 1801. He was 39 yrs old.	1801
His daughter Keziah Meade was born. 1805-1840. William was 43 yrs old.	1805
William B. Enlisted in the Civil War 1812. Gray Beard Company he was a wagon master. He was 50 yrs old. (June 18, 1812 - March 13, 1815)	1812
William B. was still in the Gray Beard Company. Fought at Ft. Defiance according to his pension letter. He was 51 yrs old.	1813
His daughter Frances Sofana Meade was born. 1814-1874. William was 52 yrs old.	1814
Civil War is over March 13, 1815	1815
His daughter Margaret Meade was born. 1817-1893. William was 55 yrs old.	1817
Mildred Ester Davis Meade Died at age 61 years old.	1830
William Bingham was living in Indiana according to his pension letter. He was 74 years old.	1836
Keziah Meade Died at age 35 years old.	1840
William Bingham Meade Sr. Died at age 79 years old.	1841
Samuel Bingham Meade Died at age 78years old.	1869
Elizabeth Meade Died at age 81years old.	1870
Margaret Meade Died at age 76 years old.	1874
William Bingham Meade Jr. Died at age 84 years old.	1883

Wm B Meade &
Isaac Brewer Jr

55 acres

Logan
&c
(— the h M Slard
apl 1st 1851

John B. Floyd — Esquire, Governor of the Commonwealth of Virginia:

To all to whom these Presents shall come—GREETING: KNOW YE, That in conformity with a survey made on the twenty third day of October, one thousand eight hundred (and forty eight, by virtue of Land Office Treasury Warrants, Nos 15830 & 17.308,

there is granted by the said Commonwealth, unto William B. Meade & Isaac Brewer Jr

a certain Tract or Parcel of Land, containing Sixty five acres, lying & being in the County of Logan, on the Left hand fork of Marrowbone creek & Jinney's creek of Sandy river, & bounded as follows, viz: Beginning at a beech & birch on the North side of said Left hand fork, thence down the fork S 29 E 97 poles to a beech on the line of said Brewer's survey; thence with the same up a branch N 42 E 24 poles to two beeches on a hill side corner to said survey S 79 E 46 poles to two poplars on a hill side N 2 E 94 poles crossing a ridge through a gap to a birch and poplar on Jinneys creek N 63 E 32 poles to a large rock; thence down said creek N 50 W 40 poles to a beech and sourwood S 44 W 34 poles to two beeches corner to said Meade's survey S 80 W 114 poles crossing said ridge, to the beginning with its Appurtenances

TO HAVE AND TO HOLD the said Tract or Parcel of Land, with its appurtenances, to the said William B. Meade & Isaac Brewer Jr and their heirs forever.

IN WITNESS WHEREOF, the said John B. Floyd Esquire, Governor of the Commonwealth of Virginia, hath hereunto set his hand, and caused the Lesser Seal of the said Commonwealth to be affixed, at Richmond, on the first day of April in the year of our Lord one thousand eight hundred and fifty and of the Commonwealth the Seventy fourth

John B. Floyd

Wm B. Meade

31 acres

Logan
4

Deld by H Anderson
Mar 18/56

Joseph Johnson Esquire, Governor of the Commonwealth of Virginia:

To all to whom these presents shall come---Greeting: KNOW YE,

That in conformity with a survey made on the *Seventh* day of *April* one thousand eight hundred and *fifty three* by virtue of Land Office Treasury Warrants, Nos *20 731 & 21,039* there is granted by the said Commonwealth, unto *William B. Meade,*

a certain Tract or Parcel of Land, containing *thirty one acres, lying in Logan County on Jenney's Creek of Sandy river, and bounded as follows, viz. Beginning at a white walnut by a cliff of rocks opposite Charles Spalden's house, lower corner to a survey made for Isaac Brewer. Thence up the hill S. 46 W. 38 poles to a hickory and birch on a ridge, S 25. E. 67 poles to a double lynn on a hill side. Due East 24 poles to a locust on steep ground S 27 E. E. 130 poles to a white oak on a hill side N. 26 W. 20 poles to a beech on a hill side N. 26 W. 206 poles to the beginning with its appurtenances*

TO HAVE AND TO HOLD the said Tract or Parcel of Land, with its appurtenances, to the said *William B. Meade* and *his* heirs forever.

In witness whereof, the said *Joseph Johnson* Esquire, Governor of the Commonwealth of Virginia, hath hereunto set his hand and caused the Lesser Seal of the said Commonwealth to be affixed, at Richmond, on the *first* day of *September* in the year of our Lord one thousand eight hundred and *fifty four* and of the Commonwealth the *Seventy ninth*

Jos. Johnson

Wm. B. Meade

Joseph Johnson   Esquire, Governor of the Commonwealth of Virginia:

To all to whom these presents shall come---GREETING: KNOW YE,

67 acres

↓

Logan

&c &c B J H Anderson

c. Mar 18 56

That in conformity with a survey made on the *eighth* day of *April* one thousand eight hundred and *fifty three* by virtue of Land Office Treasury Warrants Nos. *20,781 +*

24,039

there is granted by the said Commonwealth, unto *William B. Meade,*

a certain Tract or Parcel of Land, containing *Sixty seven acres lying in Logan County, on the ridge between the Big Laurel branch of Marrowbone Creek & the Laurel fork of Pigeon Creek, and bounded as follows, viz: Beginning at a chestnut & hickory near the line of said Meades survey of 25 acres: thence S 85 E 20 poles to a gum & hickory, N. 53. E. 134 poles to a white oak and chestnut on a ridge by a cliff S. E. 24 poles to two white oaks on the dividing ridge between said Creeks N 17 E. 62 poles to a double poplar N I W. 12 poles to a maple, corner to a survey made for John Sartain N 3 E 78 poles to two beeches by a branch N 52 W 16 poles to a white oak on the foot of a hill. S 33. W 220 poles to the beginning with its appurtenances*

TO HAVE AND TO HOLD the said Tract or Parcel of Land, with its appurtenances, to the said

William B. Meade

and *his* heirs forever.

IN WITNESS WHEREOF, the said *Joseph Johnson* Esquire Governor of the Commonwealth of Virginia, hath hereunto set his hand and caused the Lesser Seal of the said Commonwealth to be affixed, at Richmond, on the *first* day of *September* in the year of our Lord one thousand eight hundred and *fifty four* and of the Commonwealth the *Seventy ninth*

Jos. Johnson

William B. Meade   John B Floyd   Esquire, Governor of the Commonwealth of Virginia:

230 acres

Logan

Co.

Deliv: to Col. Morgan
June 1st/52

To all to whom these Presents shall come---GREETING: KNOW YE,

That in conformity with a survey made on the twentieth day of June one thousand eight hundred and fifty by virtue of Land Office Treasury Warrants Nos 17862 15 791. 17896 17895 there is granted by the said Commonwealth, unto William B. Meade

a certain Tract or Parcel of Land, containing two hundred and thirty acres lying in Logan County, on Marrow bone creek of Sandy river and bounded as follows. Viz: Beginning at an ash & red oak on a hill side near the creek lick, thence crossing the creek N 29 E 18 p° to a beech & cucumber on a hill side, thence up the creek N 68 E 56 p° to a gum & dogwood at the mouth of Little Laurel branch N 31 E 54 p° to a beech & maple N 48 E 130 p° to a beech & pine N 31 E 40 p° to a pine and maple S 80 E 48 p° to two sugar trees N 40 E 100 p° to two hickories N 80 E 108 p° to a beech N 55 E 38 p° to two beeches on the double lick branch by a lick. Thence up said branch N 82 E 40 p° to a beech N 63 E 36 p° to a beech S 74 E 11 p° to an ironwood N 78 E 42 p° to an ash thence S 16 E 18 p° to a dog wood & chisnut oak S 53 W 62 p° to a poplar S 33 E 18 p° crossing a ridge to a poplar thence up the ridge N 86 E 26 p° to a gum & poplar N 49 E 39 p° to double maple thence down double lick branch S 50 E 56 p° to a beech and gum S 85 W 56 p° to two lynns S 70 W 50 p° to a beech N 78 W 64 p° crossing the creek at the mouth of said branch to a walnut on a hill side. Thence down the creek S 64 W 150 p° to a gum S 48 W 52 p° to a double beech S 82 W 24 p° to a beech N 78 W 36 p° to a pine on the bush branch. Thence down same S 9 E 24 p° crossing the creek to a stake. S 61 W 270 p° to the beginning with its appurtenances

TO HAVE AND TO HOLD the said Tract or Parcel of Land, with its appurtenances, to the said William B. Meade and his heirs forever.

IN WITNESS WHEREOF, the said John B. Floyd Esquire, Governor of the Commonwealth of Virginia, hath hereunto set his hand and caused the Lesser Seal of the said Commonwealth to be affixed, at Richmond, on the first day of August in the year of our Lord one thousand eight hundred and fifty one and of the Commonwealth the Seventy sixth

John B Floyd

William B. Meade   John B. Floyd   Esquire, Governor of the Commonwealth of *Virginia*:

To all to whom these Presents shall come---GREETING: KNOW YE,

85 acres

Logan
&c.
Deliv. to Col. Morgan
June 1/52

That in conformity with a survey made on the *twentieth* day of *June* one thousand eight hundred and *fifty* by virtue of Land Office Treasury Warrant No. *17862*

there is granted by the said Commonwealth, unto   *William B. Meade*

a certain Tract or Parcel of Land, containing *Eighty five acres,* lying in the County of *Logan,* on the Cub branch of Marrowbone creek and Senecys creek waters of Sandy river, and bounded as follows, viz: — Beginning at a white oak & chesnut oak near a gap in the ridge between the Cub branch & Neely branches of Marrow bone creek. Thence up the ridge N 72 E 20 p⁵ to gum N 36 E 56 p⁵ to a maple N 66 W 81 p⁵ to a chesnut in a gap N 23 W 72 p⁵ to a white oak & hickory at 74 E 56 p⁵ to a poplar & hickory N 7 E 122 p⁵ to a chesnut near the swelled hickory gap in said ridge N 75 W 50 p⁵ to a chesnut oak S 27 E 34 p⁵ to a chesnut S 31 W 42 p⁵ to a chesnut S 3 W 34 p⁵ to a chesnut S 56 W 40 p⁵ to a chesnut S 15 E 210 p⁵ to the beginning, with its appurtenances

TO HAVE AND TO HOLD the said Tract or Parcel of Land, with its appurtenances, to the said *William B. Meade* and *his* heirs forever.

IN WITNESS WHEREOF, the said *John B. Floyd* Esquire, Governor of the Commonwealth of Virginia, hath hereunto set his hand and caused the Lesser Seal of the said Commonwealth to be affixed, at Richmond, on the *first* day of *August* in the year of our Lord one thousand eight hundred and *fifty one* and of the Commonwealth the *Seventy-sixth*

John B. Floyd

715

William B. Meade John B. Floyd, Esquire, Governor of the Commonwealth of Virginia:

To all to whom these Presents shall come—GREETING: KNOW YE, That in conformity with a survey made on the *fourteenth* day of *October*, one thousand eight hundred and *forty eight*, by virtue of Land Office *warrant* *Warrant, No. 15,794*

there is granted by the said Commonwealth, unto *William B. Meade,*

25 acres

Logan

(Deliv'd to M'Ward
Apl 1st 1851)

a certain Tract or Parcel of Land, containing *twenty five acres, lying and being in the County of Logan, on the ridge between Marrowbone creek with Little Laurel fork of Laurel fork of Pigeon creek; waters of Sandy river & bounded as follows, viz: Beginning at a maple and white oak at the head of the Right hand fork of the Big Laurel branch of Marrowbone creek; thence S.75.E.27 poles, crossing the ridge to a poplar on a point; thence up the ridge N.19.E. 73 poles to a white oak and dogwood N.79.E. 48 poles to two hickories N.7.E. 24 poles to a poplar; thence down the ridge N.78.W.30 poles to a poplar & hickory S.50.W.34 poles to a hickory and poplar. S.19. W. 91 poles to the beginning with its appurtenances*

TO HAVE AND TO HOLD the said Tract or Parcel of Land, with its appurtenances, to the said
William B. Meade
and *his* heirs forever.

IN WITNESS WHEREOF, the said *John B Floyd* Esquire, Governor of the Commonwealth of Virginia, hath hereunto set his hand, and caused the Lesser Seal of the said Commonwealth to be affixed, at Richmond, on the *first* day of *April* in the year of our Lord one thousand eight hundred and *fifty* and of the Commonwealth the *Seventy fourth.*

John B. Floyd

William Smith Esquire, Governor of the Commonwealth of Virginia:

To all to whom these Presents shall come—GREETING: KNOW YE, That in conformity with a survey made on the twentieth day of November, one thousand eight hundred and forty seven, by virtue of Land Office Treasury Warrants Nos. 16,498 16,702 there is granted by the said Commonwealth, unto William B. Meade

a certain Tract or Parcel of Land, containing two hundred and nineteen Acres, lying and being in the County of Logan on Jenny's Creek of Sandy river & bounded as follows Viz. Beginning at a rock and small poplar on the point on the lower side of the ... Honey branch, and corner to Survey made for Samuel Brewer, thence up said Creek S.13.E.52 poles to a large poplar and birch in a hollow N.72.E.52 poles to two small birches S.67.E.58 poles to a birch and large oak S.2.W.00 poles to a dogwood, chesnut and white Walnut S.88.E.44 poles to a lynn N.35.W.56 poles to a birch and ash N.73.W.54 poles to a large poplar N.23.W.66 poles to two birches N.52.E.65 poles to a birch S.35.E.44 poles to a large poplar S.05.E.78 poles to a birch S.30.E.77 poles to a lynn N.33.E.49 poles to a lynn and cucumber N.56.W.156 poles to two chesnut oaks on a point N.10.W.20 poles to a poplar and birch N.49.E.66 poles to a large birch on a hill side S.53.E.76 poles to two birches S.56.E.26 poles to a hornbeam S.13.W.30 poles to a Sugar tree S.43.E.34 poles to a double lynn S.33.E.56 poles to a sugar tree and Spanish oak S.52.E.38 poles to a birch S.30.E.83 poles to a birch S.12.E.06 poles to a birch N.40.W.114 poles to a birch; N.31.W.124 poles to a stake N.83.W.169 poles to a white Oak S.81.E.84 poles, crossing Upper honey branch to two birches N.56.W.66 poles to two birches S.6.W.79 poles to a large poplar and birch N.35.W.25 poles to two birches S.39.W.156 poles to a hornwood and birch S.71.W.66 poles to two birches S.15.E.89 poles to the beginning with its appurtenances

TO HAVE AND TO HOLD the said Tract or Parcel of Land, with its appurtenances, to the said William B. Meade and his heirs forever.

IN WITNESS WHEREOF, the said William Smith Esquire, Governor of the Commonwealth of Virginia, hath hereunto set his hand, and caused the Lesser Seal of the said Commonwealth to be affixed, at Richmond, on the thirty first day of August in the year of our Lord one thousand eight hundred and forty eight and of the Commonwealth the seventy third.

Wm Smith

51

William Smith Esquire, Governor of the Commonwealth of Virginia:

To all to whom these Presents shall come—Greeting: KNOW YE, That in conformity with a survey made on the *Eleventh* day of *October*, one thousand eight-hundred *and forty six*, by *virtue of Land Office Treasury Warrants No.* No. 7918

there is granted by the said Commonwealth, unto *William B. Meade*,

a certain Tract or Parcel of Land, containing *one hundred and six acres, lying and being in the County of Logan, on the ridge between the two Laurel branches of Marrowbone Creek of Sandy river, and bounded as follows, Viz.* Beginning at a poplar and red Oaks, thence down said ridge N.15° W. 50 poles to a red Oak on a point N.81.W.40 poles to two beeches on a bench N.49.W.24 poles to two beeches N.15.W.54 poles to a black gum on a point S.60.W.72 poles to a double Service tree and Sourwood on the top of the ridge N.81.W.52 poles to a white Walnut by a fall N.44.W. 70 poles to an ash on the end of a flat. S.70.W.20 poles to a beech S.85° W.36 poles to a poplar and white Oak S.5°.E.28 poles crossing a ridge to a bunch of maples S.41.W.34 poles to two white Oaks S.23.W.58 poles to a Sugar tree due West 30 poles to two white Walnuts by a branch N.58.W.80 poles to a white Oak and Sourwood S.42.W.18 poles to a spruce pine S.76.E.80 poles to a cucumber tree due East 36 poles to two beeches on a point N.25.E.40 poles to a white Oak N.41.E.50 poles to a white Oak on a ridge S.25.E.44 poles to a beech on a flat S.20. W.16 poles to two white Oaks & hickory S.74.E.32 poles to a black Oak N.56.E.20 poles to a chesnut N.72.E.84 poles to a double lynn S.5.E. 20 poles to a lynn and gum. S.21.E.46 poles to three chesnut Oaks on a flat point S.70.E.422 poles to the beginning with its appurtenances

TO HAVE AND TO HOLD the said Tract or Parcel of Land, with its appurtenances, to the said *William B. Meade*

and *his* heirs forever.

IN WITNESS WHEREOF, the said *William Smith* Esquire, Governor of the Commonwealth of Virginia, hath hereunto set his hand, and caused the Lesser Seal of the said Commonwealth to be affixed, at Richmond, on the *thirty first* day of *November* in the year of our Lord one thousand eight hundred and *forty seven*. and of the Commonwealth the *Seventy Second*

Wm. Smith

William P. Meade &c. *William Smith* Esquire, Governor of the Commonwealth of Virginia:

To all to whom these Presents shall come—GREETING: KNOW YE, That in conformity with a survey made on the *tenth* day of *October*, one thousand eight hundred *and forty one*, by virtue of *Land Office Treasury Warrant No. 5579*.

there is granted by the said Commonwealth, unto *William P Meade*

William P. Meade

70 acres

Logan County

Dilis to lot Magan
17th Mar. 1848

a certain Tract or Parcel of Land, containing *Seventy acres, lying and being in the County of Logan on the Big Laurel branch of Marrowbone Out of Sandy river, and bounded as follows viz. Beginning at an ash and hickory on the side of a knot on the ridge at the head of said branch thence N. 65° W. 72 poles, crossing a branch, to a buck & hickory N.5.E. 48 poles to a black oak N.77.E. 64 poles to two hickories on a point N.11 E. 40 poles to two hickories in the head of a drain in the edge of a flat N 85 W. 18 poles to a locust S.24.W. 54 poles to a Sugar tree and hickory on a point due South 74 poles to a hickory and buck S.51.W. 64 poles to a Chesnut and white Oak near the top of a flat ridge, S.45.E. 72 poles to two Chesnut Oaks on a point S.50.E. 20 poles to a black Oak and chesnut S.43.E. 126 poles to a buck and hickory N. 5.W. 110 poles to the beginning with its appurtenances*

TO HAVE AND TO HOLD the said Tract or Parcel of Land, with its appurtenances, to the said *William P. Meade*

and *his* heirs forever.

IN WITNESS WHEREOF, the said *William Smith* Esquire, Governor of the Commonwealth of Virginia, hath hereunto set his hand, and caused the Lesser Seal of the said Commonwealth to be affixed, at Richmond, on the *thirtieth* day of *November* in the year of our Lord one thousand eight hundred and *forty Seven* and of the Commonwealth the *Seventy Second*

Wm Smith

(William B. Meade)

William Smith **Esquire, Governor of the Commonwealth of Virginia:**

To all to whom these Presents shall come—Greeting: KNOW YE, That in conformity with a survey made on the *tenth* day of *October, one thousand eight hundred and forty six,* by virtue of *Land Office Treasury Warrants Nos. 15594 & 16064*

37 acres
&
Logan County
&c
Del'd to Col. Morgan
17th Mar. 1848

there is granted by the said Commonwealth, unto *William B. Meade*

a certain Tract or Parcel of Land, containing *thirty seven acres,* lying *and being in the County of Logan, on the Left hand fork of the Big Laurel branch of Marrowbone Creek of Sandy River, and bounded as follows, viz: Beginning at a beech, lynn and poplar at the mouth of a drain near the mouth of a big right hand hollow of Leadford. thence S. 45. W. 18 poles to a sugar tree N. 32. W. 46 poles to a beech N. 50. W. 20 poles to a white Oak and gum due South 20 poles to a maple, S. 57. E. 38 poles to a beech N. 84. E. 36 poles to an ash & beech N. 61. E. 20 poles to a hickory N. 25. W. 46 poles to a chesnut Oak & hickory on a flat point N. 78. W. 20 poles to a hickory on a point, S. 43. W. 36 poles to a black gum and maple on a flat point N. 28. W. 22 poles to chesnut Oaks on the top of a point N. 10. E. 23 poles to a hickory and chesnut N. 41. E. 38 poles to a birch on a cliff of rocks on the top of a mountain S. 35. E. 72 poles to two beeches, S. 27. E. 18 poles to a white Oak, S. 25. W. 16 poles to a poplar and beech S. 53. W. 104 poles to the beginning with its appurtenances*

TO HAVE AND TO HOLD the said *Tract or Parcel of Land,* with its appurtenances, to the said *William B. Meade* and *his* heirs forever. **In witness whereof,** the said *William Smith* **Esquire, Governor** of the Commonwealth of Virginia, hath hereunto set his hand, and caused the Lesser Seal of the said Commonwealth to be affixed, at Richmond, on the *thirtieth* day of *November* in the year of our Lord one thousand eight hundred and *forty seven* and of the Commonwealth the *Seventy Second*

Wm Smith

54

William Smith Esquire, Governor of the Commonwealth of Virginia:

To all to whom these Presents shall come—GREETING: KNOW YE, That in conformity with a survey made on the *twentieth* day of *May*, one thousand eight hundred and *forty seven*, by virtue of Land Office Treasury Warrants Nos: 11,171 & 15,419, there is granted by the said Commonwealth, unto *William Meade Jr.*

a certain Tract or Parcel of Land, containing *thirty eight acres*, lying and being in the County of *Logan*, on Hensley's big branch of Pigeon Creek of Sandy river and bounded as follows. Viz: Beginning at a white Oak & hickory on the top of a point on the lower side of said branch; thence down the point S 15 W 40 poles to two dogwoods and beech on said point; thence up the branch N 80 E 40 poles to a sugar tree N 67 E 140 poles to a gum, white Oak & dogwood in a chain S 10 E 34 poles, crossing the branch, to a large poplar on a hill side N 55 E 50 poles to a birch; thence up the Right hand fork, due East 50 poles to two birches and two beeches, N 62 E 36 poles to a beech and sugar tree on the bank of the branch, thence down the same N 83 W 104 poles to two ironwoods and chestnut sapling on the bank of the Left hand fork N 35 W 16 poles to a beech on a point S 86 W 32 poles to a large white Oak and gum in the head of a chain, S 75 W 162 poles to the beginning with its appurtenances.

TO HAVE AND TO HOLD the said Tract or Parcel of Land, with its appurtenances, to the said *William Meade Jr* and *his* heirs forever.

IN WITNESS WHEREOF, the said *William Smith* Esquire, Governor of the Commonwealth of Virginia, hath hereunto set his hand, and caused the Lesser Seal of the said Commonwealth to be affixed, at Richmond, on the *thirty first* day of *August* in the year of our Lord one thousand eight hundred and *forty eight* and of the Commonwealth the *Twenty third*

Wm Smith

William B. Meade John B. Floyd Esquire, Governor of the Commonwealth of Virginia:

To all to whom these Presents shall come---Greeting: KNOW YE,

That in conformity with a survey made on the *twentieth* day of *June* one thousand eight hundred and *fifty* by virtue of Land Office Treasury Warrant No. *17862*

there is granted by the said Commonwealth, unto *William B. Meade*

85 acres

Logan
&c

Deliv'd to Col. Morgan
June 1/52

a certain Tract or Parcel of Land, containing *Eighty five acres, lying in the County of Logan, on the Cub branch of Marrowbone creek and Senney's creek, waters of Sandy river, and bounded as follows. viz: Beginning at a white oak & chesnut oak near a gap in the ridge between the Cub branch & Neely branches of Marrow bone creek Thence up the ridge N 72 E 20 p° to gum N 36 E 86 p° to a maple N 66 W 81 p° to a chesnut in a gap N 23 W 42 p° to a white oak & hickory at 74 E 86 p° to a poplar & hickory N 76 E 122 p° to a chesnut near the swelled hickory gap in said ridge N 75 W 30 p° to a chesnut oak S 27 E 34 p° to a chesnut S 31 W 42 p° to a chesnut S 3 W 34 p° to a chesnut S 56 W 46 p° to a chesnut S 15 E 210 p° to the beginning, with its appurtenances*

TO HAVE AND TO HOLD the said Tract or Parcel of Land, with its appurtenances, to the said

William B. Meade

and *his* heirs forever.

In witness whereof, the said *John B. Floyd* Esquire, Governor of the Commonwealth of Virginia, hath hereunto set *his* hand and caused the Lesser Seal of the said Commonwealth to be affixed, at Richmond, on the *first* day of *August* in the year of our Lord one thousand eight hundred and *fifty one* and of the Commonwealth the *Seventy-sixth*

John B. Floyd

seventy one in the Eleventh year of our Reign.

Ex:

Wm Nelson P.

John and Lawrence
163 Acres
Form page

George the third &c. To all &c. Know ye that for divers good causes &
Considerations but more especially for and in Consideration of
the Sum of Twenty shillings of good and lawful money for our
Use paid to our Receiver General of our Revenues in this our Colony
and Dominion of Virginia We have given granted and confirmed
and by these presents for us our heirs and Successors Do give
grant and confirm unto John Lawrence and Paul Lawrence one
certain tract or parcel of Land containing one hundred & sixty
three acres lying and being in the County of Nansemond on
the East side of Blackwater river and bounded as followeth, to
wit, Beginning at a Pine at the head of a small branch thence
running East forty six Poles to a red Oak standing in the Patent line
thence along the said Line South one hundred and thirty six Poles to a
corner Gum thence bounding on the said Patent line West one hundred
and ninety four Poles to an Oak North one hundred and thirty six
Poles to a Pine East ninety Poles to an Oak in the branch aforesaid
and thence up the said branch to the beginning The same being
surplus Land found within the bounds of a Patent for eight hundred
and thirty acres granted to George Lawrence the twenty seventh day
of April one thousand six hundred and eighty six With all &c. To have
hold &c. To be held &c. Yielding and paying &c. Provided &c. In Witness
&c. Witness our trusty and welbeloved William Nelson Esquire President
of our Council and Commander in Chief of our said Colony & Dominion
at Williamsburg under the seal of our said Colony the sixteenth day
of February one thousand seven hundred and seventy one, in the
eleventh year of our Reign.

Ex:

Wm Nelson P.

(c)

William Meade
520 Acres
Form pages

George the third &c. To all &c. Know ye that for divers good causes and
Considerations but more especially for and in consideration of the sum
of fifty five shillings of good and lawful money for our use paid to
our Receiver General of our Revenues in this our Colony and Dominion
of Virginia We have given granted and confirmed and by these
Presents for us our heirs and Successors Do give grant & confirm

unto

…grant and Confirm unto Richard Hello one certain Tract or parcel of Land Containing three hundred acres lying and being in the County of Southampton on the North side of Black Creek and bounded as followeth. To wit. Beginning at a white Oak a corner of Robert Mongers land thence North fifteen degrees East ninety eight poles to a pine then North sixty degrees East fifty two poles to a red Oak then North seventy five degrees East ninety six poles to a white Oak ... ... thence East one hundred and thirty four poles to a pine, then South forty degrees East one hundred and twenty poles to a white Oak then South, South West one hundred and fifteen poles to a Lightwood Stake in Joseph Bradshaw's line thence by the said Bradshaw's lines North seventy five degrees West sixty seven poles to a red Oak South eighty degrees West forty two poles to a white Oak a corner of Robert Mongers land aforesaid thence by the said Monger's lines North seventy degrees West one hundred and fifty five poles to a red Oak West thirty eight poles to a white Oak and then South seventy degrees West forty four poles to the Beginning With all &c. To have held &c. To be held &c. Yielding and paying &c. Provided &c. In Witness &c. Witness our trusty and well beloved John Earl of Dunmore our Lieutenant and Governor General of our said Colony and Dominion at Williamsburg under the seal of our said Colony the fifth day of July one thousand seven hundred and seventy four in the fourteenth year of our Reign.

E₊ a   Dunmore

George the third &c. To all &c. Know ye that for divers good Causes and Considerations but more especially for and in Consideration of the Sum of Four pounds of good and lawful Money for our use paid to our Receiver General of our Revenues in this our Colony and Dominion of Virginia We have Given Granted and Confirmed and by these presents for us our heirs and Successors Do Give Grant and Confirm unto William Meade one certain Tract or

parcel

Land-Office Military Warrant, No. 3842

To the principal SURVEYOR of the Land, set apart for the Officers and Soldiers of the Commonwealth of Virginia.

THIS shall be your WARRANT to survey and lay off in one or more surveys, for John Mead Heir at Law of William Mead, dec'd his Heirs or Assigns; the Quantity of Two Thousand Six hundred sixty six & two thirds Acres of Land, due unto the said John Mead dec'd in consideration of sd Wm Mead Services for three Years as an Ensign in the Virginia Continental Line agreeably to a Certificate from the Governor and Council, which is received into the Land-Office. GIVEN under my Hand, and Seal of the said Office, this 29 Day of April in the Year One Thousand Seven Hundred and 85

Land Office Military WARRANT, No. 3842.

To the principal SURVEYOR of the Lands set apart for the Officers and Soldiers of the Commonwealth of VIRGINIA.

THIS shall be your WARRANT to survey and lay off in one or more Surveys, for John Mead Heir at Law to William Mead Dec'd his Heirs or Assigns, the Quantity of Two Thousand Six Hundred Sixty six 2/3 Acres of Land, due unto the said John Mead said William Mead dec'd In consideration of his services for Three years as an Ensign in the Virginia Continental line agreeable to a Certificate from the Governor and Council received in the Land-Office. GIVEN under my Hand, and the Seal of the said Office this 29th Day of April in the Year One Thousand Seven Hundred and 85

Jno Hawkins S. Off

Land-Office Military Warrant, No. 3664

To the principal SURVEYOR of the Land, set apart for the Officers and Soldiers of the Commonwealth of Virginia.

THIS shall be your WARRANT to survey and lay off in one or more Surveys, for Wm Mead ass'ee of Jno Perrin his Heirs or Assigns; the Quantity of one hundred Acres of Land, due unto the said Wm Mead Perrins In consideration of John Services for three years as a soldier in the Virginia continental line agreeably to a Certificate from the Governor and Council, which is received into the Land-Office. GIVEN under my Hand, and Seal of the said Office, this 1st Day of ___ in the Year One Thousand Seven Hundred and 85

59

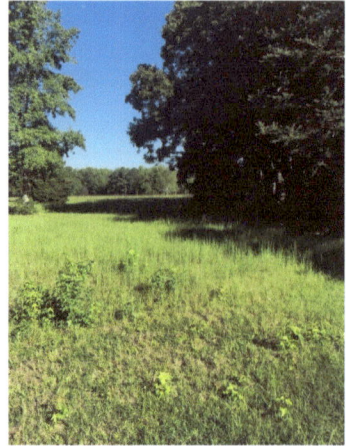

Cowpens Battlefield
Elaine Meddings 2016

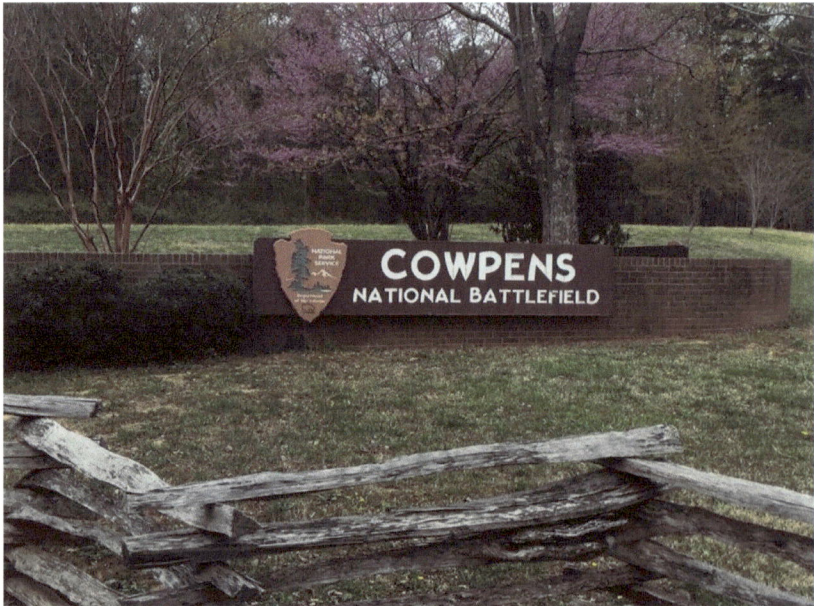

President Franklin D. Roosevelt signed the Executive Order 6166, on June 1933. This order transfered the national military parks and national battle-field sites from the War Department to the National Park Service in the De-partment of the Interior. Until 1933 Cowpens was just a battlefield site. Then in 1970 Cowpens was expanded into a major national battlefield.

*William Bingham Meade Jr. and
Jane Ellen Rutherford*

*William Bingham Meade Jr.
and Jane Ellen Rutherford*

William Bingham Meade, III
1843-1937

*William Bingham Meade III
and Eveline Brewer*

Explanation of the Meade Coat of Arms

Gold [Or] Generosity   **Red** [Gule]
Courage

Black [Sable] Nobility   **Silver** [Argent]
Sincerity

Blue [Azure]

The Pelican among the Egyptians was symbolic of the four Peternal duties, viz, Generation- Preservation – and good example. According to tradition Pelicans picked their own breast to norish their young.

The Pelican's in the crest are wounding themselves for their young. So the House Of Meade is thought minded of their Children so very much that they are for them to their own hurt.

Mead is the English from the Norman "de Prato" and to say that a Family is Norman is equivalent to saying it is among the oldest of the old, and noblest of the Noble.

Motto: Semper Paratus - - Always Ready.

The Norman "de Parte" was translated into English, Meade, Mead, Mede and Medes. The House of Meade (Mede) was one of the People of ancient media, a kingdom in what is now northwestern Persia, which attained its greatest power in 700-600 B.C.

The Meade Families are all related if you go back to 1066, they came to England from Normandy and France. The Families who settled in Ireland dropped the [E] – to Mead, and the English retained it in most cases, some did leave it off, it being usually picked up in the next generation.

The Meades [Meds] came to Normandy, when they were released from bondae, by the Egyptians. Prior to that they were a strong nation of their own, 700 to 600 B.C.

The Meade Families of Kentucky and West Virginia are Quakers and are members of the "Hopewell Community of Virginia".

There is no established relationship between the Mead and Meade families of Kentucky and West Virginia although they seemed to communicate with each as they left Virginia and North Carolina at about the same time and settled near each other in Kentucky and West Virginia. It appears the Quaker Mead's stopped and visited with the William Bingham Meade family at Fort Vancouver, (Now Fort Gay, West Virginia).

The coat of arms is thus described:

Sa. A Chevron between the three pelicans or vuln. Gu.

Explanation: Sa., the color is sable, /e., black

The Chevron –

A chevron represented as two rafters of a house joined together and decending in the form of a pair of compasses to the extremities of the shield. Or., signifies gold, and in engraving is represented by dots.

Three pelicans vuln. Gu., /.c, wounding themselves, according to the old traditions that the pelicans picked it's own breast to nourish it's young.

Crest, and eagle displayed.

Motto: Semper Paratus – Always Ready

State of Indiana,
Jennings County, ss.

On the 18th day of July
1836 before me the subscriber a Justice of the Peace for the said County
of Jennings personally appeared
William Meade of said County
who on his oath declares that he
is the same person who formerly belong-
ed to the company commanded
by Captain George Baker in the
Regiment commanded by Colonel
Benjamin Cleaveland in the
service of the United States; that
his name was placed on the Pension
Roll of the State of Virginia from
whence he had lately removed; that
he now resides in the State of
Indiana where he intends to
remain, and wishes his pension
to be payable in future The following
are his reasons for removing from
Virginia to Indiana — I am
very old & infirm and have removed
to Jennings County Indiana where
my sons resides

William Meade

Sworn to and
subscribed before
me the day & year
aforesaid

David Elliott
Justice of the Peace

To the onorable secertary of war in the highest
gretting sir after my greatest submvison to your
onner j have rote the gentleman of virgina
for a transfer to Draw my money in the State of
indiana at the town of mattison that Bank
Sir j have sent twice the first time by the mattsen
town paymaster to the
petioners that give each solder there money returnd
not done rigt and sent a paper to fill out wich
was done a long time and got no anser pray sir
forward a answer gennings County State of indiana
j was famly of grinup County Centucy State sent
to you from there then j carried by water to gen County
State of virginea where j sent you my proof agin for
there is a good many of my name but do not spell
there name as j do they are namesakes but no kin
to me they do not put my last letter William Meade
there Mead and Meed but no kind to Me j was
Born in fudrick County State of virgina first volterd
under william thomas milisha Captain then
listed under gorge baker a recruting offiser under
Benyamin Cleavland Colonel then ordered
to go to the aid of danel Morgen and faugt under
the virginia line with him at the Cow pens or above
them a little.

there I was severely wounded in my head five peaces of
my skull bone took out from my head and wounded
in my leg and my right brest wounded with the
baonett and suffered hunger and naked and cold
joined in the last war with briton termed in my old
years to old to muster for some years but joind
the grey beard Company and served a honerable
tower of duty done to fort defeance on the bank
of the maighme river near fort wane in the year of 1813
... sir I am a very infirm man and be oblige to move
with my sone to the state of indiana where I expect
to stay the remained of my life I wish to draw
my pay heree in indiana sir I am very foale and old
I stil have the consumption spiting blood and muley
I first woat by thompson ward comerdand
ing general and gustis of the peace of grimes county
Centucky state deare sir you grated my ... watere and
sent it by the barer joseph stratton candidate
for logan county state of virginia excus my riting
my hand is cripled so that I can only mark you no my
prof is good pray god sir have mercy on a old solder
and sufer me a transfer to mattison town bank
this from your most humbel servent of William Meade
to the honerable secrritary of war in my Case October the
sir send a few lines mattison post offis 3rd day 1836.
jinning county indianna state I have been ill used
about my money in virginia logan county by old
Antony loson who run the post office

Page 9 - **Lt. Colonel John Edgar Howard**,
Painted in 1782 by Charles Willson Peale.
Public Domain Wikimedia

Nathanael Green,
by Charles Wilson Peale 1783,
Public Domain

Cowpens Battlefield by Elaine Meddings

Page 10 - **Andrew Pickens**, from Wikipedia, the Free
Encyclopedia. (1739-1817). Google Images.
Permission CCBYSA 2.5 Wikimedia

Cowpens Battlefield by Elaine Meddings

Rebecca Calhoun, Anonymous Brown,
Wikitree, Google Images.

Page 11 - **Cowpens Battlefield** by Elaine Meddings

Cowpens Battlefield by Elaine Meddings

Banastre Tarleton, by Sir Joshua Reyonalds,
National Portrait Gallery, London,
Public Domain, File: Created 31, December
1781 Wikimedia.

Page 12– **Mary Robinson** by Thomas Gainsborough
Originally from wikipedia Public Domain
Created: 31 December 1780.

Page 18 - **Cowpens Battlefield** by Elaine Meddings

Cowpens Battlefield by Elaine Meddings

Page 19 - **Cowpens Battlefield** by Elaine Meddings

Cowpens Battlefield by Elaine Meddings

Page 20 - **Cowpens Battlefield** by Elaine Meddings

Cowpens Battlefield by Elaine Meddings

Page 21 - **Cowpens Battlefield** by Elaine Meddings

Cowpens Battlefield by Elaine Meddings

Page 22 - **Cowpens Battlefield** by Elaine Meddings

Cowpens Battlefield by Elaine Meddings

Page 23 - **Cowpens Battlefield** by Elaine Meddings

Cowpens Battlefield by Elaine Meddings

Page 24 - **Cowpens Battlefield** by Elaine Meddings

Cowpens Battlefield by Elaine Meddings

Page 25 - **Cowpens Battlefield** by Elaine Meddings

Cowpens Battlefield by Elaine Meddings

Library of Congress
Ancestry.com
U.S. Census Records 1700's and 1800's
West Virginia Death Index 1853—1973
Revolutionary War Pension Records

William Meade (Mead)
Pension Application S19394 FN 39 NC

AMERICAN FORCES

BRIGADIER GENERAL DANIEL MORGAN, VIRGINIA, COMMANDANT
MAJOR EDWARD GILES, MARYLAND STATE REGIMENT, A.D.C.
BARON DE GLASBEECH, VOLUNTEER, A.D.C.

CONTINENTAL TROOPS

THE LIGHT INFANTRY, MARYLAND LINE,
CONTINENTAL ESTABLISHMENT
290 MEN

LIEUTENANT COLONEL JOHN EAGER HOWARD,
MARYLAND, COMMANDANT
BENJAMIN BROOKES, MARYLAND,
CAPTAIN AND BRIGADE MAJOR
CAPTAIN ROBERT KIRKWOOD, DELAWARE

MARYLAND	MARYLAND
CAPT. RICHARD ANDERSON	ENSIGN WALTER DYER
CAPT. HENRY DOBSON	ENSIGN SMITH
LIEUT. JAMES EWING	VIRGINIA
LIEUT. GASSAWAY WATKINS	LIEUTENANT BARNES
	LIEUTENANT MILLER
LIEUT. SAMUEL HANSON	ENSIGN KING

THIRD REGIMENT, LIGHT DRAGOONS
80 MEN

LIEUTENANT COLONEL WILLIAM WASHINGTON,
VIRGINIA, COMMANDANT
MAJOR RICHARD GALL, VIRGINIA
CAPTAIN WILLIAM BARRET, NORTH CAROLINA
LIEUTENANT HENRY BELL, VIRGINIA
CORNET JAMES SIMONS, SOUTH CAROLINA
LIEUTENANT THOMAS ANDERSON,
MARYLAND, VOLUNTEER

MILITIA TROOPS

COLONEL ANDREW PICKENS,
SOUTH CAROLINA, COMMANDANT
MAJOR JAMES JACKSON,
GEORGIA, BRIGADE MAJOR

VIRGINIA	GEORGIA
200 MEN	100 MEN
MAJOR GEORGE TRIPLETT	MAJ. JOHN CUNNINGHAM
CAPTAIN TATE	CAPT. SAMUEL HAMMOND
CAPTAIN BUCHANAN	CAPT. GEORGE WALTON
CAPTAIN GILMORE	CAPT. JOSHUA INMAN
ENSIGN COMBS	NORTH CAROLINA
ENSIGN McCORKILL	140 MEN
ENSIGN WILSON	MAJ. JOSEPH McDOWELL

SOUTH CAROLINA
115 MEN

COLONEL THOMAS BRANDON
COLONEL JOHN THOMAS, JR.
COLONEL JOSEPH HAYS

SOUTH CAROLINA HORSEMEN
45 MEN

COLONEL JAMES McCALL,
COMMANDANT

TOTAL AMERICANS 970 MEN

BRITISH FORCES

LIEUTENANT COLONEL BANASTRE TARLETON COMMANDANT

TARLETON'S LEGION	550 MEN
7TH REGIMENT MAJ. NEWMARSH	200 MEN
1ST BATTALION OF THE 71ST REGIMENT MAJ. McARTHUR	200 MEN
DETACHMENT OF THE 17TH REGIMENT OF DRAGOONS	50 MEN
DETACHMENT OF THE ROYAL ARTILLERY	50 MEN
TOTAL BRITISH	1050 MEN

NAMES.	Rank.	Annual allow-ance.	Sums re-ceived	Description of service.	When placed on the pension roll.	Commencement of pension.	Ages	Laws under which inscribed, increased, and reduced; and remarks.
Philip Ballard	Private	80 00	168 00	Virginia contin'l	Dec. 24, 1833	Mar. 4, 1831	77	Died April 13, 1833.
John Cook	do	80 00	137 08	New York militia	Nov. 30, 1833	do	80	Died Nov. 21, 1832.
William Davis	do	80 00	200 00	Virginia contin'l	May 23, 1833	do	87	
William Davis	do	80 00	240 00	Va. State troops	May 19, 1834	do	78	
William Meade	do	80 00	-	Virginia militia	Ap'l 28, 1834	do	72	
Ralph Stewart	do	20 00	-	do	do	do	84	
Robert White	do	80 00	240 00	Va. State troops	Nov. 21, 1833	do	79	
Oliver Walker	do	20 00	60 00	Virginia militia	Apr. 4, 1834	do	89	

William Bingham Sr Mead in the Abstract of Graves of Revolutionary Patriots

Name: William Bingham Sr Mead

Cemetery: Pigeon Creek Cem

Location: Mingo Co WV 66

William Bingham Meade

BIRTH 1762-08-22 • ,Frederick,Maryland,USA

DEATH 1841-02-11 • ,Logan,Virginia,USA

Facts

Birth
1762-08-22 • ,Frederick,Maryland,USA

Marriage
30 Dec 1769 • Wilkes, North Carolina, USA
Mildred Ester Davis (1766–1841)

Birth of Sister Arnstead Meade (1770–)
1770

Birth of Brother John Mead (1770–1825)
12 Oct 1770 • Bedford, Bedford, Virginia, United States

Birth of Brother Samuel Meade (1770–1828)
12 Oct 1770 • Virginia, United States

Sources

Ancestry Sources

1810 United States Federal Census

1820 United States Federal Census

1830 United States Federal Census

1840 United States Federal Census

Abstract of Graves of Revolutionary Patriots

American Genealogical-Biographical Index (AGBI)

Ancestry Family Trees

Family

Parents

Robert Meade
1743–1825

Hannah Rhodes
1750–1855

Spouse & Children

Mildred Ester Davis
1766–1841

Elizabeth Meade Brewer 1789–1886

Samual Meade
1791–1860

Margaret Meade
1793–1812

Anna Meade 1794–1830

William Bingham Meade 1798–1902

Birth of Brother Benjamin Meade (1772–1821)
14 Mar 1772 • Bedford, Bedford, Virginia, United States

Birth of Sister Edy Meade (1774–1849)
1774 • Bedford, Bedford, Virginia, United States

Birth of Brother Rueben Meade (1774–1843)
17 Feb 1774 • Bedford, Bedford, Virginia, United States

Birth of Brother Rhodes MEAD Sr (1775–1843)
6 Dec 1775 • Bedford, Bedford, Virginia, United States

Birth of Brother Robert Meade (1775–1833)
6 Dec 1775

Birth of Daughter Elizabeth Meade Brewer (1789–1886)
04 Oct 1789 • Wilkes, North Carolina, USA

Birth of Daughter Elizabeth Meade (1789–1886)
4 Oct 1789 • Wilkes, North Carolina, United States

London, England, Church of England Deaths and Burials, 1813-1980

North Carolina, Compiled Census and Census Substitutes Index, 1790-1890

U.S. Pensioners, 1818-1872

U.S., Find A Grave Index, 1600s-Current

U.S., Revolutionary War Pension and Bounty-Land Warrant Application Files, 1800-1900

U.S., Revolutionary War Rolls, 1775-1783

U.S., War of 1812 Service Records, 1812-1815

Virginia, Compiled Census and Census Substitutes Index, 1607-1890

John Meade 1800–

James E. Meade 1803–

Adam Monroe Sr Mead 1806–1863

Anna Meade Burges 1812–

Frances Sofanna Fanny Meade 1814–1876

Spouse & Children

Elizabeth Meade 1789–1886

Samuel Meade 1791–

Marriage
30 Dec 1789 • Wilkes, North
Carolina, United States
  Mildred Ester Davis
  (1766–1841)

Birth of Son Samual Meade
(1791–1860)
1791 • Wilkes, North Carolina, United States

Birth of Son Samuel Meade
(1791–)
1791 • Wilkes, North Carolina, United States

**Birth of Daughter Margaret
Meade** (1793–1812)
1793

**Birth of Daughter Anna
Meade** (1794–1830)
1794 • Fort Vancouver, Logan, Virginia, USA

**Birth of Son William Bing-
ham Meade** (1798–1902)
25 Apr 1798 • Bedford, Bedford, Virginia, United States

Birth of Son John Meade
(1800–)
1800 • Fort Vancouver, Logan, Virginia, United States

Web: West Virginia,
Find A Grave Index,
1780-2012

Birth of Son James E. Meade
(1803–)
1803

**Birth of Son Adam Monroe
Sr Mead** (1806–1863)
1806 • Virginia, USA

Residence
1810 • Frederick, Virginia,
United States

**Birth of Daughter Anna
Meade Burges** (1812–)
1812

Military
1812 • United States

Residence
1812 • Guiford County Regiment, NC

**Death of Daughter Margaret
Meade** (1793–1812)
1812

**Birth of Daughter Frances
Sofanna Fanny Meade** (1814
–1876)
1814

Residence
1820 • Floyd, Kentucky,
United States

Death of Brother Benjamin Meade (1772–1821)
19 Apr 1821 • Tygart Valley, Greenup, Kentucky, United States

Death of Father Robert Meade (1743–1825)
Jan 1825 • Harold, Floyd, Kentucky, United States

Death of Brother John Mead (1770–1825)
1825 • Floyd, Georgia, United States

Death of Brother Samuel Meade (1770–1828)
1828 • Floyd, Kentucky, United States

Residence
1830 • Eastern District, Frederick, Virginia, USA

Death of Daughter Anna Meade (1794–1830)
1830 • Logan, Logan, West Virginia, USA

Military
1833-1849 • Virginia, US

Death of Brother Robert Meade (1775–1833)
1833

Residence
1834 • North Carolina

Residence
1840 • Cabell, Virginia, United States

Death of Wife Mildred Ester
Davis (1766–1841)
11 Feb 1841 • ,Logan Wv,,

Death
1841-02-11 • ,Logan,Virgin-
ia,USA

Burial
25 Jul 1841 • Kermit, Mingo
County, West Virginia

Marriage
, Wilkes, North Carolina, USA

  Mildred Ester Davis
  (1766–1841)

Residence
North Carolina, United
States

Residence
VA, United States

Marriage
,Wilkes,North Carolina,USA

  Mildred Ester Davis
  (1766–1841)